8-1-19 1 Hr
8-2-19 1 Hr
9.04-19 1 HR -
9-05-19 1 hr.   3:30-4:30pm Thurs.
9-06-19 1 hr.   3:30-4:30pm Fri

La Fredrick D. Smith

www.lafredrickdsmith.com

Teach in the Name of Love

Building Relationship with Students

LaFredrick D. Smith

Teach in the Name of Love
Copyright © 2017 by LaFredrick Smith
All rights reserved.

Published by lafredrickdsmith.com
In the United States of America

ISBN: 9781521576489

DEDICATION

This book is dedicated to my very first class ever, the Class of 2023 at KIPP Legacy Preparatory School. I know I was there to be you all's teacher, but you all taught me more than I could ever teach you. Thank you all for teaching me and pushing me to connect with each of you. You all will forever be my students. Especially my mini-me Jacques!

"Every child deserves a champion - an adult who will never give up on them, who understands the power of connection and insists that they become the best that they can possibly be."

- Rita F. Pierson

Table of Contents

"Teaching is not about information. It's about having an honest intellectual relationship with your students."

\- Paul Lockhart

Introduction

I am that "WHY" teacher! The teacher that everyone always looks at and just says, "WHY." I seem to get asked this all of the time by fellow educators, parents, and even students from other classes. They want to know why I care so much, or why I put so much effort into connecting with my students, or why I do so much for my students. The answer is my experiences. Most people do things based on their previous life experiences and mine have molded me into the teacher I am today.

As a student in grade school, I wasn't the "perfect student" that all teachers hope to have in their classes. You know, the students that are respectful, do their homework, ask questions, show all strategies, etc. I was that student that required some extra attention. I was that student that needed the most love. Many teachers wouldn't put up with me and provide me with that love I needed, but there were a few that put in the effort to make a connection with me. They went above and beyond to ensure that I was successful, not just academically but all around. These teachers were my great examples of "WHY" teachers. These are the teachers that helped shape me into the educator I am today.

I'm going to start in high school and work my way backward, you'll understand in a moment.

In high school, I had two teachers who truly had an impact on my life. The first was my sociology/psychology teacher. This lady really knew how to connect with her students. She was that teacher who knew what to say and how to say it to let her students know she was on their level. I looked forward to going to her class every day just because I knew she would have an engaging lesson that would keep me focused and willing to learn. You would think that was the case in all classes, but it wasn't. She connected with students in a way to let them know that she not only cared about them academically, but that she also cared about them as a human being. I remember one day her phone rang in class and her ring tone was "Big Poppa" by The Notorious B.I.G., the entire class turned up. Those were the types of moments that made her class special, and that made her relationships with students unique.

The next teacher in my high school life was my tenth-grade math teacher. This teacher is the definition of "above and beyond." Her class was towards the end of the day, and as a high school boy, two hours after lunch, you get a little hungry. Now keep in mind that I was not the best student. Even in my favorite teacher's classes, I still was not on my best behavior. This teacher connected with me through food. Each day I entered her classroom, before math instruction would start, she would allow me to go behind her desk and get a Diet Dr. Pepper and some Cheddar Flavored Pretzels. I think it was almost every day that I had this snack in her class. I know she bought this snack for herself, but I feel like she always got a little extra just for me. Even when she was not in attendance, the substitute knew that it was okay for me to get my snack. Most teachers won't even let you eat in their classroom, and this woman had a snack for me every day. If that didn't make me want to learn math, I don't know what else would have. Even though it was just a small snack, she was my champion that school year.

I'm going to end with my kindergarten teacher. I'm ending with her because she made the last real impact I had as a grade school student. I don't remember kindergarten well, but I do remember my teacher. She not only taught me, but she also taught all of my siblings. She kept in contact with our family each year after we left her class. When you live in a small town, you run into your teachers all of the time. This teacher here is a true example of what it means to build long lasting relationships with your students. I remember this moment like it was yesterday; it was my high school graduation. The announcer had just said my name, and I was walking across the stage, shaking hands and smiling. As I was leaving the stage, I saw a woman standing there smiling. Guess who it was? My kindergarten teacher. She was standing there with her arms open for a hug, with a card in her hand. That card had two pictures on it, one from when I was a kindergarten student, and then one of me as a senior in high school. The card read, "I was there when you "took off" on your way through school. I've watched you grade by grade, always "climbing." Congratulations on your graduation from High school. Soar even higher – always reaching for your goals. – Your kindergarten teacher." Now, that's how you make an impact.

I'm that "WHY" teacher, the teacher that everyone always asks the question "WHY" to. I am that teacher because of the teachers I had. I have taken the way they connected with me and use their methods in my classroom each and every day. I want to leave the same impact on my students that those teachers left on me. I am intentional about connecting with my students as human beings, I go above and beyond for my students each day, and I want to be that teacher at the end of the stage celebrating my students for each of their successes. I want to be their biggest fan, their champion teacher. My teachers connected with me during my years in their classes, but those connections have had a lasting impact on my life and forever will. These teachers taught me in the name of love, and I will go into my classroom every day teaching my students in the name of love.

As you read this book, keep in mind that these are Mr. Smith's ways of building relationships with students. Use them as motivation and direction in finding ways that fit your classroom and teaching style. I hope you enjoy reading and good luck at connecting with your students.

"No Significant learning
can occur without a
significant relationship."

- James Comer

It's a MUST! Building Relationships with Students!

"I wrote this blog about two years ago when I first realized the key to success in my classroom... building relationships. Ever since this day, I knew what my niche was and have focused on it ever since. I started with this blog, just to give you an overview of the importance of relationships in the classroom."

- L. Smith

I have just wrapped up my first semester of my 2nd year of teaching. Over the summer I read many books, attended professional development workshops, and watched many videos in order to grow and prepare myself for a successful school year. All of those things were great, and I feel as if they have really prepared me to be an awesome teacher this school year. One thing that I didn't learn more about, but should have (and so should all teachers) was building relationships with students to ensure a successful school year. Without relationships and connections in the classrooms, effective learning will not happen.

Why is it so IMPORTANT?

#1 Students need to know that you care about them – When you take the time out to get to know each of your students and build a strong, positive relationship with them, it gives them assurance that you care about them.

#2 Students trust you – Building relationships with the students also builds a level of trust between you and the student. The students know that you care and that you are here for them, and they begin to trust you with their hearts and brains.

#3 Student achievement grows – Once students know that you care about them, you are here for them, and there is trust, they begin to work harder for you. Once you start to build relationships with the student and they understand your purpose (to teach and to care), they begin to find their purpose (to learn).

Mr. Smith's Tips

#1 Get to know each student individually – Getting to know each student, lets the students know that you care about them as a person and it helps you understand them more.

#2 Treat all students the same – Being fair and consistent helps the students understand your purpose and will allow them to trust you more.

#3 Promises are sacred – The students want to trust you and will always do their part if you do your part.

#4 Have open communication – Build a culture with the students where everyone can communicate respectfully and openly. The students want to be able to tell you things, but if you come off as unapproachable, they won't communicate with you.

#5 Be human – Let the students know that you are human just like them. If you make a mistake, own it. If you are upset, say it. Showing them that you're human, will help them open up more and trust you.

"By building relationships, teachers can transform futures."

- Rachel Garfield

Before the School Year Starts

When building relationships with students, many people believe that it's something that just happens or that it's not a top priority when having a successful classroom. Contrary to popular belief, building relationships is just as important as planning an effective lesson. It actually should be thought out and planned just as we intentionally plan lessons for our students.

Before the school year starts, I intentionally start to build relationships with students. Many of my students know me, know of me, or has heard from me in some way before the first day of school. These few things make my classroom run so much smoother and ensures that my school year is off to a successful start.

Ending with Relationships

The end of the school year is always a fun time. Classroom celebrations, graduations, sharing memories, etc. This time of the year is also perfect to start building relationships with your future students.

As a 4th-grade teacher, I would step into the 3rd-grade classrooms. Start by learning the student's names and speaking to them on a daily basis. Then move into having small conversations with them at lunch or during dismissal. You may not know who exactly will be in your class the next year, but it doesn't hurt to get to know all of the students.

The students get really excited to know that you have an interest in them. They'll start to see you as someone that cares and will slowly begin to build that connection. This sends them into the summer with the next grade level and their new teachers fresh on their mind. They'll be anticipating all summer long to know if you will be their teacher or not!

Welcome Letters in the Mail

Once I get my class roster in hand, I immediately begin to write welcome letters. I hand-write each student a welcome letter (something small as a postcard will do fine), showing them how excited I am to have them in my class for the upcoming school year. THEY LOVE IT!

I wish I was actually there to see the smiles on their faces when their parents inform them that they have mail, and they open it up to see that their new teacher has written them a note. What better way to show students that you care than a personal note.

Parent Phone Calls

Most parents don't enjoy getting phone calls from teachers. They automatically assume that you're calling to inform them that their child is misbehaving. They are probably even more confused when they receive a phone call from their child's new teacher during the summer.

Just as we have to build relationships with our students, we have to build them with the parents too. After all, this is a three-way relationship; the teacher, the student, and the parent.

Each year, I take the time out to call each parent on my roster and simply welcome them and their child to my class for the upcoming school year. This is also a great opportunity to invite parents to meet the teacher night (you could use a postcard for that too). Just as the students get excited to receive a letter from their teacher, the parents are equally excited to receive a phone call.

The saying is students need to know that we care before they learn from us. I believe the same goes for parents. Your parents need to know that you care about their child before they can fully support your classroom. Once you get your parents on board, life is so much easier.

"It's the little conversations
that build relationships
and make an impact on
each student."

- Robert John Meehan

During the School Year

Now that we have covered what to do before the school year starts, we can move on into the school year. After the letters home and phone calls to parents, you should be able to start the year with strong connections. However, that means nothing if you don't keep up those relationships.

Working in low-socioeconomic schools many students have hard times connecting with adults, they struggle with trusting others, and they may not realize that you care until the last day of school. We have to ensure that we are working on those relationships even when we don't want to and be purposeful about connecting with those students.

These are a few things I do during the school year to intentionally build relationships with all students, especially those hard to reach students.

Knowing Students Beyond the Classroom

How well do you really know your students? When building relationships, we have to get to know our students beyond how they perform in class or how they behave during recess. We have to learn to connect with our students beyond the classroom.

Our students want us to be interested in them. They want us to know their likes and dislikes and to be honest. Knowing our students beyond the classroom will allow us as teachers to know them more academically.

I spend a lot of my extra time at school focusing on getting to know my students. I want to know what they do for fun, what they do when they get home, how many siblings they have, and even their living situation. This allows me to better understand why they may have certain actions in the classroom, and show them that I am interested in them on a level beyond the classroom.

This can be done in many ways! I simply stop by the cafeteria and sit with a few students each day at the beginning of the school year or chat with students while at recess. They love the conversations and feel as if they are superstars giving an interview.

High Expectations and Fresh Starts

We all know that students aren't perfect. Neither are we! Just like we may talk in a meeting when we aren't supposed to or drive above the speed limit when no one is watching, our students have similar actions in the classrooms. It's OKAY! Everyone messes up. We can't allow small things our students do to cause us to hinder a relationship from being built.

We must be able to hold our students to those expectations and allow them to start fresh each day with a clean slate. Yes, they may get on our nerves and make us want to scream, but the feeling is probably mutual. When our students do things that are less desirable, we have to hold them to high expectations, give the feedback on how to improve and welcome them back with open arms. This lets them know that you may not have liked their behavior, but you care enough about them to push them into the right direction.

Sports, Recitals, and Birthdays

This one right here really keeps those relationships going throughout the year. Our students are involved in so much outside of school, and the thing they love the most is when they see their teacher sitting in the bleachers or watching from the sidelines at one of their sports events or performances. They really enjoy seeing their teachers walk up to their birthday party, if even for a minute.

Now, this may seem just a bit extra, but trust me, your students will talk about it for weeks to everyone they come in contact with.

Showing a student that you care about them so much that you take a few moments out of your day to support and cheer them on, will have that student working 10x harder in the classroom to show you that they care in return.

Holidays and Class Celebrations

Holidays and class celebrations are great ways to show students that you care and to allow them to see another side of you that they may not see when you are in teacher mode.

No, you don't have to go out and spend all of your money or be extra fancy. Just a little something from your heart to let your student know that you care. I love holidays and decorating. For each holiday or season, I put something up to make my students experience magic when entering my classroom. However, Christmas is my favorite. My students love to see the Christmas tree put up and they love it even more when I begin to place presents underneath it. No, every child doesn't deserve a gift, nor did they bring you a gift, and their behavior probably hasn't been a gift either. But, we have to learn to put that stuff to the side for the sake of relationships and connecting with students.

Class parties are my absolute favorite. This is an opportunity to turn on some music and celebrate with your students. The celebration can be over anything you choose, normally academic or behavior. During that celebration, step out of your comfort zone and try the new dance the students are doing or join in and sing the song that is playing. They will love it, and it will bring you all closer together.

Nicknames and Handshakes

A special nickname or handshake is an excellent way to build and keep relationshps with students who are hard to connect with.

Students love when their teacher creates something special just for them, and to be honest, it may be easier to remember a nickname that you have created for a student rather than their real name at the beginning of the year.

These names and handshakes don't have to be extreme, just something small to let students know that you care enough to do something special for them. An easy way to do this is to ask students what they want to be when they grow up and call them by that name... Dr. so and so.... The students will absolutely love it, and the connections between student and teacher will grow stronger.

"I call my students my kids, because in our time together they are not just names on a class list; they become a part of my heart."

\- Unknown

After the School Year

I am a strong believer in LONG LASTING relationships. I feel that every student needs that teacher that they know will always be there for them. I may just be crazy, but I had a teacher that kept up with me all the way until high school graduation, and I want to be able to do the same for my students.

Being able to continue relationships with your students even after the school year ends is one of the most amazing things ever. When students know they have someone like you cheering them on, they are sure to go all the way to the top!

Movies and Updates

Many of us always tell our students how we will keep in contact with them even after they leave our class, but how many of us really do that once the new school year starts and we have a whole new set of students? It can be really hard to ensure that we are maintaining those long lasting relationships and really keeping up with our students.

One way I ensure this happens is through scheduled activities with my old students. Now, I don't do this with every single student I have ever taught, but I do keep up with the majority of them. Over the summer, I may get a few students and take them out to see a movie or to a local education event in town, then afterward we will go to an eating place of their choice (normally

McDonalds or Chick-Fil-A) and just talk about how things are going.

My students really enjoy it, and I always tell them it may happen, so when they see you pop up at their door, they are really shocked.

Short Story: about two years ago at one of my lunch room chats with a student, he was telling me how he really loved the movie "The Purge." I had an interest in the movie as well. I told that student if they ever made a new one, we would go to the movies to see it (not knowing they were making a new one that summer). When he heard about the new movie coming out, he reminded me of what I said on the last day of school. I just smiled and agreed! One random day that summer, I contacted his parents to let them know I was going to take him and some other students to see the movie.

They choose not to tell him, to make it a surprise. So, when I rung the door bell, he answered the door and was literally blown away to see his teacher there ready for the movies. THE END!

Moments like that will have a lasting impact on your students and forever make them remember you.

Graduations and Celebrations

A great way of connecting with students and fostering that long-lasting relationship is to make an effort to attend those students' graduations and celebrations.

If you remember from the introduction about how my teacher was there at my high school graduation, then you would understand why this small action can be impactful and memorable.

No need for gifts or anything special. This is a situation where your presence is your present. Your students will be so excited to see your face sitting in the audience there to support them.

More Postcards

One last thing I love to do is send random postcards to my old students. They really enjoy getting these in the mail or at the schools. They don't have to say much, just something to let them know you remember them and still support their dreams.

I normally do this around state testing time to let my old students know that I believe in their abilities to do great. They love reading these right before the exam, and I'm sure they are even more motivated than before reading them.

Birthdays would also be another great time to send them, but that may get out of hand as the years go on.

Mr. Smith's Back to School Bash

Now, remember the things in this book are what Mr. Smith does to build relationships, and you should do what works best for your classroom and teaching style.

A few years ago, I decided to start a back to school bash for my students. The idea came about when I decided to move schools and knew I wouldn't have the opportunity to see my old students on the regular.

The back to school bash was open to all students. However, it was specifically geared towards my former students. At the bash, there was food, music, games, and each student went home with schools supplies for the next year.

This is one of my favorite things to do that continues to foster long-lasting relationships with my students.

My vision is ten years from now, the back to school bash in still happening, but instead of just passing out school supplies to my former students, I will be able to hand out college scholarships to them and help make some of their impossible dreams, possible.

"Students don't care how much you know, until they know how much you care."

\- John C. Maxwell

First 15 Days of Building Relationships

The first days of school are the most crucial in ensuring that you are connecting with students and getting those relationships off to a great start. I am a strong believer that relationships are intentional and must be planned out to ensure that they are effective. Just as I sit and plan my lessons for each year, month, week, and day, I do the same for how I am going to build relationships with my students. I want to ensure that I am not getting so focused on instruction that I leave out the most important part, relationships!

Day 1 – Have student name tags on the desk before they walk in. Put their name on one side and a special note on the other. This shows students that you cared enough before they even got to your class to have a seat ready for them.

Day 2 – Have students complete an interest survey. Don't just have them complete it, just to be doing it. But, have them complete it and turn it into a discussion. Then file it in their folders so that you can refer to it often. This shows students that you are interested in who they are as people.

Day 3 – Have students complete a multiple intelligence activity. This is a quiz/survey that shows the students and teachers what type of learners they are. This shows the students that you are invested in meeting their needs this school year.

Day 4 – Have a class discussion about what the students want to be when they grow up and assist them with setting goals. This lets students know that you care about their future and will also help you to start creating some nicknames.

Day 5 – By this day, all student names should be memorized. I know this seems small, but students really do feel some type of way when the teacher is still asking, "What is your name?" or still looking at the name tags.

Day 6 – This is a great day to start popping into the students' lunch period. For students who seem harder to connect with, go and sit next to them for a few minutes and just talk to them about their hobbies.

Day 7 - Tell a joke in class today or do something funny. You have to let your students know that you are human too. This will help them connect with you more and feel more comfortable in your classroom.

Day 8 – At recess, jump into a game with the students or have a race with them. Having connections outside of the classroom will allow students to connect with you more and feel more comfortable around you.

Day 9 – Make some type of promise to the students. "At the end of today, we will have a dance party if everyone…." Then honor that promise. Promises are sacred, and for students who may struggle with trusting adults, this will show them that you are trustworthy and can keep your promises. This will open up a line of communication for some of your students who may not have connected with you yet.

Day 10 – Welcome the students to class with personal notes from you about a success the student has had. This will let the students know that you care about their success in your classroom.

Day 11 – Call home or send a note home to parents to let them know the progress of their child so far. This allows you to connect with parents on a good note at the beginning of the year.

Day 12 – Share a story with your students that may relate to some of their lives. This allows you to make more connections to students that are harder to connect with and to make some of the connection you already have stronger.

Day 13 – Start working on some handshakes or secret codes with the students. They're going to love it, I promise!

Day 14 – Share with students how you feel about them so far. Be sure to be honest and share the good and the bad. This will let students know that you are there to celebrate their successes, but you are also there to make them better people.

Day 15 – Provide students an opportunity to share how they feel about the classroom and you as a teacher. This can be done in a morning/afternoon meeting, a survey, a writing prompt, or whatever works for you.

This allows students to share with you for means of improvement and to let them know that you care about their opinion and that it is worth something in your classroom.

"Great teachers focus not on compliance, but on connections and relationships."

\- PJ Caposey

Success Stories

Here you will find a few success stories about students I've had in my classroom and how building relationships with them led them to great success.

Success Story #1

My first year teaching happened in an unusual way. I was actually a teacher fellow in a kindergarten classroom with an experienced teacher learning the ropes. A teacher decided that they needed to leave for personal reasons and that left a 4th-grade class teacher-less. I was asked, and I decided to step up to the challenge and entered the classroom as those students' teacher. I went in the following weekend and redecorated the classroom, got materials together, and studied up on my new students. That Monday I went into the classroom and was more excited than ever to meet those students.

I was welcomed by a young lady who had looped with the teacher who had left and did not want another teacher. She walked into the classroom and began to voice her opinion about how she didn't want me there and how she hated how I decorated the classroom. For weeks we didn't connect. We had some issue almost every day. She would come in, make a class disruption, and I would put her out. The cycle would just continue.

It started to get tiring dealing with her, and she wasn't progressing academically. Something had to happen! An opportunity came about at this golfing camp. I was able to pick one student from my class to take each weekend for a month. I had many students who I already build a relationship with that I could have taken, but instead, I took her.

Over the next month, each Saturday for two hours we went to the golfing camp. After each session, I would take her to Chick-Fil-A, and we would eat and chat. During those chats, I learned so much about her. I learned about her home life, her academic struggles, and her social struggles. We were able to talk through some stuff and ended up finding a real connection.

That year she scored in the advanced level on the state assessment. I now see her in the local H-E-B or when I go to visit their school. She continues to tell everyone that I am her favorite teacher. I worked so hard to build a relationship with this student that I also ended up building one with her younger brother. It warms my heart every time he sees me and runs to me with a big hug.

Success Story #2

This next student also came from the class described in the success story above (yes, I was in a unique classroom). This young man was known for his behavior issues. Before I even got to the class, I had multiple interactions with the student in the hallway when he wasn't following the expectations. His behavior didn't change when I entered the room either; it got worse.

I remember this moment like it was yesterday. I was standing at the front of the class getting ready to teach the math lesson.

When I looked up, he was laying on top of the desk with his arms out like an airplane. He paired this action with airplane noises. The entire time I was thinking, *"What have I gotten myself into?"*

This student needed a different kind of love, and I struggled to find a way to give it to him. It was tough love that finally got us connected. I would have to sit him out at recess, followed up by many parent phone calls.

Those time outs at recess or sitting with the teacher at lunch was the best thing that happened to us. During those times, we were able to chat and really got to know one another.

At the end of the school year when the state assessment scores came back in, I pulled him to the side and asked him how he thought he did. He responded, "I probably did horrible, because my behavior has been bad all year." I showed him his results, and he passed every single assessment. He jumped for joy, shouting with excitement and stated, "Thank you Mr. Smith for being so hard on me this year and making me focus."

Success Story #3

This next student didn't really have any major behavior issues. He actually connected with me from day one and has never left my side. He is my true example of fostering those long-lasting relationships. All throughout the year, this student would work extremely hard. When asked why, he would always say, "To make Mr. Smith proud."

On the last day of school, I had just finished telling the class that I would be moving on to a new school, and he was upset because he was moving schools as well and would be leaving all of his friends. As the bell rang, I gave my goodbyes and hugs and sent the students to their dismissal areas. He continued to come back crying saying he didn't want to leave. We both ended up shedding tears in the middle of the hallway until he finally left.

I continued our long-lasting relationship by visiting his new school for lunch or inviting him to the movies so that he has an opportunity to see his old friends. He enjoys every moment of it, and I enjoy knowing that I am making a positive impact on his life.

Success Story #4

I will end the success stories with a young man that has a special place in my heart. My first time seeing this young man was in the hallway when he was going back and forth with another teacher. At that moment, I knew I wanted to take that young man under my wing. He wasn't even in my class or grade level, but something told me to connect with him.

I started to drop by his classroom and check-in on him or stop by his lunch time to see how things were going. We slowly built a connection, and our conversations began to grow. The dreams he would tell me and the goals he would share were so amazing. He even had a love for reading that no one knew about because he didn't want others to know that he enjoyed books.

Now, I'm not saying he became the perfect student overnight. He continued to have struggles, and some of his behavior grew. However, it was amazing how he would immediately calm down when I walked in or would request to come to my classroom for a cool down moment.

I took this young man under my wing and ensured his school year was successful. I saw him grow from a troubled student to someone who could have a bright future.

His classroom teacher stated how she had looped with this student for three years and that the year I built a relationship with him was the year he made the most growth ever. She continues to thank me for taking the time out to reach him.

There are many more success stories that I could have shared, and there are many more that I will gain over my years as an educator. I chose these stories to exemplify the beauty of building relationships with students and putting the extra time and effort in for powerful connections.

"Students work hardest for teachers they like and respect."

- Dr. Debbie Silver

Tips for Building Relationships

Show students you care by:

- Giving them a personal greeting each day when they arrive.

- Asking about their feelings, e.g., dialogue journals.

- Asking about their life outside of school, e.g., listening bear.

- Listening to them.

- Eating in the cafeteria occasionally with students.

- Recognizing birthdays in some way.

- Sending cards and positive messages home, e.g., happy grams.

- Finding out about their hobbies and special talents, e.g., interest surveys.

- Making home visits.

- Sharing something personal about yourself.
- Spending time playing with them — at recess or during free classroom time.
- Establishing positive relationships with every child regardless of their academic or social abilities.
- Getting to know their parents through home visits and classroom meetings.
- Calling parents periodically to report their child's success or accomplishments.

Show students you believe in them by:
- Identifying negative self-talk.
- Promoting positive self-talk.
- Communicating your belief that they can succeed.
- Making "I can" cans out of empty juice cans and drop strips of paper in them on which students have written skills they

have learned, e.g., math facts, spelling words, sharing with others, helping. (This is also useful to show parents the child's progress.)

- Making phone calls to students to applaud their special efforts or accomplishments.
- Helping every child in the classroom to appreciate other's special talents and needs.
- Following their lead, listening carefully to their ideas, and being an "appreciate audience" at times.

Show students you trust them by:
- Inviting students to help with daily tasks and classroom responsibilities.
- Offering curriculum choices.

- Encouraging collaboration among students.
- Encouraging students to help each other.
- Sharing your thoughts and feelings with them.

Reference:
Teacher Classroom Management
© *The Incredible Years*®

"The key to a successful classroom is the relationships built with students."

- LaFredrick Smith

Appendices

Sample Welcome Letter

Dear Students and Families,

Welcome to [grade/class]! I'm super excited about the opportunity to get to have you in my class this year, and I'm looking forward to a happy and productive school year.

Students are asked to bring the following supplies to school before [date]: [supplies].

Special classroom events planned for the year include [international day, medieval night, poetry readings, etc.]

Upcoming school events you should be aware of include [dates of open house, conferences, book sale, welcome luncheon, etc.]

Please mark those dates on your calendar. Studies show that parental involvement in a child's education is one of the strongest indicators of student achievement. We hope you will make it a priority this year to attend as many school-sponsored events as possible.

If you have any questions or concerns or if you would like to visit our classroom, schedule a conference, or volunteer to help out, you can contact me at [contact info]. The best times to reach me are [available hours].

Once again, welcome to [grade/class]. Let's work together to make this the best year ever!

Sincerely,

[Your name]

Parent Phone Call Script

Hello, is this the parent of _____?

This is _____, I am your child's ____ grade teacher.

I am calling to welcome you all to the new school year!

We have open house on _____ and I would love to see you all in attendance.

Do you have any questions for me?

Thank you, and once again, welcome to _____ classroom!

Student Interest Survey

1. The three things that I do best in school are…

2. Some of the things that I would like to work on this year are…

3. I would like to learn more about…

4. Outside of school, my favorite activity is…

5. My hobbies are…

6. The clubs, organizations or private lessons that I participate in are…

7. My favorite sport is…

8. The sports that I play in and out of school are…

9. My three favorite books are…

10. One of my favorite authors is…

11. If I could choose between watching television, playing video games or using the computer, I would…

12. The person that I consider to be a hero is…

13. If I could pick a place to travel to, I would choose…

14. Some of the chores and responsibilities that I have at home are…

15. Three of my friends are…

16. Something about me that I'd like to share with you is…

95475461R00050

Made in the USA
Lexington, KY
09 August 2018